Activity Workbook for
When My Baba ♥ My Yiayia Died

Marjorie Kunch

PASCHA PRESS

Educate Edify Entertain

Copyright © 2017 Marjorie Kunch

All rights reserved. No part of this publication may be reproduced or transmitted in any form or by any means electronic or mechanical, including photocopy, recording, or any storage and retrieval system now known or to be invented without prior written permission from the publisher or author.

Pascha Press

Toll-free telephone: 1-844-4-PASCHA

http://www.paschapress.com

This publication is designed to provide accurate information, for general purposes only, in regard to the subject matter covered. There are no warranties or representations, expressed or implied. It is sold with the understanding that the publisher and author are not engaged in rendering legal, medical, or other professional services. If legal advice or other expert assistance is required, the services of a competent professional person should be sought.

ISBN: 978-0-9964045-0-1

Bible quotes from the KJV and sourced from the public domain

Clip art used with permission by ofc.org and sourced from the public domain

Coloring pages: original artwork inspired by images from www.dce.oca.org and kind permission granted for use by Ftr. John Matusiak

Koliva image: acoantioquena.com

Prayer for the departed: orthodoxprayer.org

Dear teachers and helpers of bereaved children,

In my 12 years serving as a funeral director across three different states, I have come across many different families and many different children. A common thread links them all-questions from both the tall and the small. The experience of a loved one dying can be potentially scary or it can be an opportunity to reinforce the loving teachings of Christ. Many times adults are working through their own grief and how it was modeled for them when children themselves, complicating how they relate to their own family. As Father Konstantinos Tsiolas wisely says in *When My Yiayia Died*, "It is up to us to give our children the Orthodox understanding of the meaning of death, not as a defeat and an end, but as Christ's victory on the Cross. It is a chance for us to teach our children about the Resurrection of Christ and His promise of eternal life in His Kingdom." Young ones need reassurance that although their loved one is no longer here in the physical sense, their memory will never be forgotten. If a child has not yet experienced a death in the family, this workbook will serve to better prepare them for that inevitable event and to cement in their minds why a funeral is so important to our Faith.

This is where the Orthodox Church excels, with our various services dedicated to our deceased loved ones. So many times the answers to questions children and adults alike seek can be found within the Church. This workbook is meant to be a companion to the previously released titles which discuss either Greek or Slavic funerary customs. These stories can be used as a tool to reinforce concepts presented in a gentle way and to broaden a child's understanding of the Faith as practiced across different Orthodox jurisdictions. To help children begin their own journey of grief accompanied by the comfort of you, the helpers in their lives, and the comfort of Christ. To quote V. Rev. Dr. Milos Vesin who kindly wrote the foreword of *When My Baba Died*, "The funeral service—and all of its components—in the Eastern Orthodox Church, is mainly about two matters: prayer, and love; two matters which never die." It is my humble prayer that these series of books, which sprung from my own personal experiences of loss, will serve to bring the reader closer to our Risen God and the comfort of the Orthodox Faith.

Your co-laborer in Christ,

Marjorie Kunch

Blessed are those who mourn, for they shall be comforted.
—Matthew 5:4

In the story, we are introduced to either a little Serbian girl or a little Greek boy who found out that their Baba or Yiayia—another term for someone's grandma—had died. Has someone in your life died, too? Perhaps you heard about a famous person who passed away, like a President or a movie star? Write their name below.

_____

- -

_____

When you learned about this person's death, how did it make you feel? **Grief** is the name we give these feelings. If grief was a thing and not a feeling, what do you think it would look like? Can you draw this object, or perhaps use different colors to show how you feel in your heart when you think about the word grief?

Write a few sentences about your grief. How did you think it would make you feel, how do you actually feel, can you write a poem about it?

Sometimes it is hard to put into words what you are feeling. You could ask your helper to show you some Bible verses or look up poems that people often read at **funerals**. Maybe copy these words down instead, if creating your own is difficult.

_____
_____
_____
_____
_____
_____
_____
_____
_____

Here are some good verses to get started, can you think of any others?

1 Corinthians 15:52-57 *Phillipians 3:20-21*
1 Peter 1:3-9 *Psalm 23*
John 14:1-4 *Revelation 21:4*

We learned that "falling asleep in the Lord" is entirely different than falling asleep at bedtime. Does this make you feel comforted, to know that Jesus promised He will "trample down death" and we will see our loved ones again? Color the icon on the next page. Maybe keep it at your bedside to remind you that you have no need to fear bedtime. God is with you and God is with your loved one, too.

God is always with us.

Ask your Mama, Papa, or any other helpers in your life to say this prayer with you:

Prayers for the Departed

Christ our eternal King and our God,
You have destroyed death and the devil by Your Cross
and have restored man to life by Your Resurrection;
give rest, Lord, to the soul of Your servant [name]
who has fallen asleep in Your Kingdom,
where there is no pain, sorrow or suffering.

In Your goodness and love for all men,
pardon all the sins he [she] has committed
in thought, word, or deed,
for there is no man or woman
who lives and sins not,
You only are without sin.

For You are the Resurrection, the Life, and Repose
of Your servant [name], departed this life,
O Christ our God; and to You do we send up glory
with Your Eternal Father and Your All-holy, Good and Life-creating Spirit;
both now and forever and to the ages of ages.

Amen

When someone dies, you will more than likely visit a funeral home for the viewing. Sometimes you will visit a church instead. Have you been to a funeral home before? Inside it looks like a larger version of your own living room, doesn't it? This is where the **visitation** usually takes place. Many people will come to talk, cry, and share happy memories of your loved one with your family.

One way to spark the sharing of our remembrances is to create a *memory table*. This is where we place things that remind us of our loved one and the accomplishments they achieved. You might use pictures of your loved one growing up or you might use a trophy they won in school. Perhaps your loved one enjoyed cooking and so you use things from their kitchen to decorate the table. Maybe you will give out copies of a recipe for cookies they baked every Nativity. Maybe they liked to fish and so you could place a few bobbers on the table. Can you think of other hobbies people enjoy and what object could be used to represent these?

What are some things you would like to use to decorate a memory table, placed either at the **funeral home** or perhaps in your own home? Write these below.

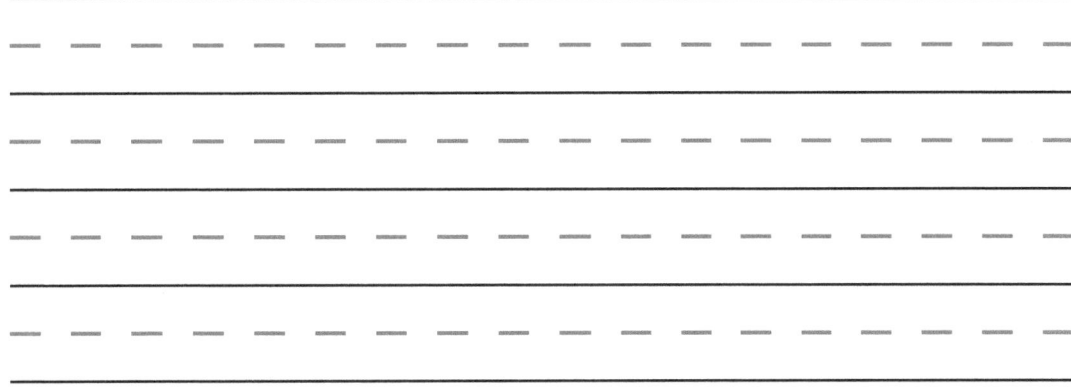

People will send flowers to show sympathy for your loss. Ask if you can take a flower home—such as a sturdy rose to hang upside down and dry or perhaps some smaller flowers to press inside pages of a book—as a keepsake. These would make a nice addition to your memory scrapbook you may wish to make for your loved one. Maybe you would like to create a collage inside of a shadowbox frame from the craft store using the memorial cards from the funeral, perhaps their picture, and the dried flowers. Ask an adult to help you glue these in place then you can hang this keepsake on your wall.

A long time ago, people kept a box called a casket hidden inside their homes. This was much like a treasure chest, only their most precious valuables would go inside. At the funeral home, we will see our loved one in a box also called a **casket**. Why do you think we chose this same word from long ago to describe something we use in the modern day? Does this teach us that we too are precious?

It is hard to remember to treat our bodies well when we are so busy planning all of the events surrounding a funeral. Remember to value your own body by taking time to eat healthy food and to drink plenty of water. Ask Mama or Papa to pack nutritious snacks to take to the visitation.

Did you know that the day after the viewing Orthodox families will bring a special dish of food to the Church? This dish is called **koliva** by Slavic families and **sitari** by Greek families. Read the definition of the term koliva or sitari in you book. Ask your helper to discuss what a "metaphor" is and how this concept relates to the verse. Here is a recipe for koliva/sitari, ask if you can help prepare it:

1 lb. Whole wheat berries (I use Bob's Red Mill from the grocery store)
2 C. Walnuts, chopped finely with a food processor
1 C. Raisins-golden or regular. Other dried fruit is fine as well.
1 C. Granulated sugar
2 tsp. Cinnamon
Pinch of ground clove
1 C. Graham cracker crumbs
1 ½ C. Powdered sugar
1 C. Slivered almonds
White Jordan almonds (if not at your local grocer, look at a party supply store or craft store in the wedding section, usually by the favors)
Small cups and spoons to distribute the koliva/sitari at the ceremony

TWO DAYS BEFORE NEEDED:
Sort the wheat berries, place in colander and rinse thoroughly in cool running water. Place rinsed berries in a large bowl and cover with additional water. Meanwhile, combine ground walnuts, raisins, cinnamon, cloves, and granulated sugar and set aside. Reserve the graham cracker crumbs, powdered sugar, and almonds for addition later.

DAY BEFORE NEEDED:
Rinse and drain the wheat berries. Add to a deep pot, roughly a 1:2 ratio of berries to water or 2½ C. berries to 5 C. water. Bring to a boil then simmer three hours, stirring frequently. You may need to add additional water. Do not overcook so that the grains burst in the pot. They should be whole, chewy, and burst between your teeth.

After three hours, drain and immediately rinse in cold water to stop the cooking process. Spread out over a large, clean towel and allow to dry for several hours. Place back into the large bowl and refrigerate until tomorrow.

MORNING OF THE SERVICE:
In a large fancy bowl to use at church, mix the wheat with the previous day's combined dry ingredients and add in the slivered almonds. Press the mixture down into the bowl with a piece of parchment or waxed paper in order to "compact" it some and give yourself a flat surface for decoration. Sprinkle with the graham cracker crumbs first to serve as a moisture barrier, then make a thick layer of powdered sugar. Use the Jordan almonds to form a cross. Some families also add the initials of the deceased as well. Remember to leave a space at the top for the candle to go. Cover with plastic wrap and head directly to church. Yields 50–60 servings.

Consume the day it is prepared, do not eat leftovers as it can ferment. Any unconsumed koliva/sitari should be treated as you would any blessed item. Sprinkle the excess someplace outdoors where it will not be trampled on.

*Very truly I tell you, unless a kernel of wheat falls to the ground and dies,
it remains only a single seed. But if it dies, it produces many seeds.*
—John 12:24

It is often helpful to leave items inside the casket of the deceased, this shows love and comforts us as well. Some children like to draw a picture of happy times spent with their loved one and place this paper inside the casket, others like to leave a copy of a family photograph. When my grandma died, I placed a teddy bear in her casket for her to keep and I kept a matching teddy bear for myself to hug whenever I missed her. Even grown-ups need to hug their teddy bear sometimes! Can you think of anything else you might do to show love? Write your answer below.

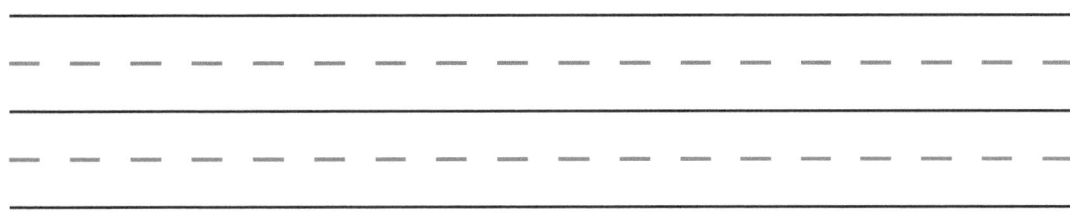

Sometimes children like to write a letter expressing how they will never forget him or her. Since this is a private letter you can seal in an envelope, is there anything you feel like you want to apologize for, or ask forgiveness? Although your loved one dying may bring feelings of guilt up, know that it is NOT YOUR FAULT they died.

Maybe you feel badly you missed their birthday and thought you would make it up "next year", which now will not happen due to their passing. Does this teach us that time is precious? Maybe you're really angry they left you. Write your letter to your loved one expressing all of your feelings, both good and bad. Also, pretend you are your loved one looking down from heaven, how do you imagine they would reply? Do you think they would say they love and forgive you? God forgives us and our loved ones will, too. They are in a place of peace and light where sadness does not exist. No matter how badly you think they felt because of a missed birthday or an unanswered phone call, it is not possible for your loved one with God to feel anything but a perfect love for you.

Any confusing feelings that you may have, though, talk to your priest either in confession or in some other meeting. It is his job to help you during this difficult time and he would be honored if you allowed him to do so. God trusts priests to do His will on Earth and so we should trust priests with our deepest feelings as well, even if it feels a bit scary to share these feelings with someone. I promise that your priest will not think badly of you, EVERYONE feels this way sometimes! You will feel much better after talking through these emotions.

Use this page to make a drawing of a happy time spent with your loved one. Keep this page to look at whenever you feel sad. Maybe copy this drawing on a separate piece of paper and place inside their casket so they can have it as well. It can be something you both share forever.

Paximadia-Greek Funeral Cookies

½ C. Butter
½ C. Crisco
1 C. Sugar
3 large eggs
1 tsp. vanilla
2 tsp. baking powder
½ tsp. baking soda
4 C. flour

Topping: ½ C. sugar mixed with 1 ½ tsp. cinnamon

Preheat oven to 350 degrees, have two cookie sheets at the ready.

In a stand mixer, cream butter, shortening, and 1 C. sugar until fluffy.

Incorporate eggs, one at a time, then add vanilla.

Sift together baking powder, baking soda, and 3 C. of the flour, add to the wet ingredients and beat until well mixed.

Gradually add remaining cup of flour until a soft dough forms (you may not need to add the full cup.)

Divide dough into four equal pieces and roll into logs.

Two logs each onto an ungreased cookie sheet, flatten down dough logs to about 2 ½ inches wide.

Bake for 10 minutes, rotate pans, then bake an additional 10 minutes.

Remove from oven, transfer to cutting board, slice on the diagonal into roughly half inch pieces.

Roll cookies in sugar-cinnamon mixture and then place back onto baking sheets, sliced side down, and bake an additional 15 minutes.

Remove pans, flip cookies over, return to oven for a final 15 minutes. Remove cookies to wire racks to cool.

VOCABULARY WORD SEARCH

Look backwards, forward, up and down!

Grief	Funeral Director	Embalmer
Church Triumphant	Funeral	Visitation
Pascha	Casket	Pomen
Priest	Trisagion	Funeral Home

```
N R C T S B E Q M U V Y O P F U N E R A L J Q D L F E I R G
E Y N Q T I P S E S W A Z C B U J M O L E A X O A W P E S M
K G U O P T W Z C B N I O Y E Q A X V F R T W L J M G B R D
P G V B N C V M L K H J P A S C H A R E B B H Y G Q W S K L
A L R T F C X Z S W E F N B O L E M O H L A R E N U F R C S
R O T C E R I D L A R E N U F P L C F O K M N B Y H U I J Q
B V G H Y U J K I V C X Z W E L P O C A S K E T L O G C E A
T W Q S X P Y J K T V X W C K O L Y S A Z W Q I O E H O D X
R W O Q X L I Z E D C F I P L Q A B N K L Q B H M X C T Y I
U P T D Q W Z D U D O P R I C L X M T E W A X Z O U Q J L B
H V A B N M I O P W Q F G H C H U R C H T R I U M P H A N T
R Y O G W X N I Y F W L C S M H W Q A I K O N X Z E R W A C
N B T R P J K I U Y H T G F S A Q W E D C V B O P R I E Z T
G T U J R P L K J H G F D S A Q W E C V B N M Y T G J I Z E
K B G F I D R T G H Y N P O M E N H G T F D S W V H B N K E
I G Y H E U K I N B V C E P O B V L E Q W S G C A S K T R E
C V F R S G H N J U Y T M N E M B A L M E R U Y G F S C R F
P A S E T B G T R E M F U N E R L A W E P R I S G F T R Q B
U Q D T V Z O P T E B W I O M Q A X V R T K L Z I R B N S Y
T R I S A G I O N F D S A Q W E E S D F N O I T A T I S I V
```

Solution to Word Search:

```
N R C T S B E Q M U V Y O P F U N E R A L J Q D L F E I R G
E Y N Q T I P S E S W A Z C B U J M O L E A X O A W P E S M
K G U O P T W Z C B N I O Y E Q A X V F R T W L J M G B R D
P G V B N C V M L K H J P A S C H A R E B B H Y G Q W S K L
A L R T F C X Z S W E F N B O L E M O H L A R E N U F R C S
R O T C E R I D L A R E N U F P L C F O K M N B Y H U I J Q
B V G H Y U J K I V C X Z W E L P O C A S K E T L O G C E A
T W Q S P Y J K T V X W C K O L Y S A Z W Q I O E H O D X
R W O Q X L I Z E D C F I P L Q A B N K L Q B H M X C T Y I
U P T D Q W Z D U D O P R I C L X M T E W A X Z O U Q J L B
H V A B N M I O P W Q F G H C H U R C H T R I U M P H A N T
R Y O G W X N I Y F W L C S M H W Q A I K O N X Z E R W A C
N B T R P J K I U Y H T G F S A Q W E D C V B O P R I E Z T
G T U J R P L K J H G F D S A Q W E C V B N M Y T G J I Z E
K B G F I D R T G H Y N P O M E N H G T F D S W V H B N K E
I G Y H E U K I N B V C E P O B V L E Q W S G C A S K T R E
C V F R S G H N J U Y T M N E M B A L M E R U Y G F S C R F
P A S E T B G T R E M F U N E R L A W E P R I S G F T R Q B
U Q D T V Z O P T E B W I O M Q A X V R T K L Z I R B N S Y
T R I S A G I O N F D S A Q W E E S D F N O I T A T I S I V
```

The morning of the funeral ceremony will be very busy. You may have to wake up earlier than you are used to and wear special clothes. This is how we pay respect to the one who has died, by being on time for the service and dressing up. It may be helpful to lay your clothes out the night before so that you don't feel as rushed.

You will have heard people say many nice things about your Baba or Yiayia at their **eulogy**. In church you will hear beautiful singing. Afterwards you will hear joyful stories of your loved one at the funeral luncheon, called a **Makaria** or mercy meal. During the funeral you will have heard about Christ and His promise of eternal life. Jesus says in His Father's house there are many mansions (John 14:2) and He goes to prepare a place for those who will meet Him in heaven. What do you think heaven is like? Draw or write below what you think your loved one sees in heaven right now.

Have you met the **funeral director** yet? This is the person who helps your family with all of the details that go into planning a funeral. The funeral director meets with bereaved families, they arrange for the visitation, write an obituary, contact clergy, request military honors for veterans and get their flag, set the room up with flowers, order the casket and vault, have memorial cards made, tell the cemetery to dig the **grave**, wash the hearse so that it is shiny for the funeral, handle insurance policies and other administrative tasks. They even get your loved one ready for their visitation. They will bathe and dress your loved one and help them to look peaceful in their casket. Sometimes, if specifically requested by the family, they will also use the art and science of **embalming**.

The funeral director is also a helper alongside clergy in their ministry to the bereaved. Many funeral directors are volunteers at civic clubs like Rotary or Lions. Some funeral directors are active in church as readers or in choir. Does it sound like a funeral director is a very busy person? I bet your funeral director isn't too busy to talk to you! Ask him or her to speak about their profession and why they chose it. Maybe your teacher could invite your local priest or funeral director to come and give a speech on career day? Maybe YOU would like to be a priest or funeral director when you grow up!

What kind of schooling do you think it takes in order to be a priest or funeral director? Look up your nearest seminary or mortuary college and view their course catalog. Write below some of the classes you discovered they would take in order to obtain his degree in Theology or his/her degree in Mortuary Science. Are there any classes you are surprised to see?

Your priest will mention the Father, the Son, and the Holy Spirit many times throughout the funeral service. This is referred to as the Trinity. Trinity means three. Write below:

A) What three things will you miss about your loved one?
B) What three things will you remember about your loved one which makes you feel happy to think upon?
C) Finally, name three things the priest in the book uses to bless Baba or Yiayia in church. Your priest will do the exact same blessings for your loved one, too, just like all Orthodox people have had done. Does this make you feel comforted to know we are all connected in this way: past, present, and future?

A) _____

B) _____

C) _____

Answers to C:

He uses a censor/incense to bless Baba's or Yiayia's casket, he blesses her body with holy oil, he blesses Baba or Yiayia with a hand cross.

The church is an important place for all of life's seasons. We are baptized here, married here, and when we die our funeral is held here. We see on page 24 of the storybook what an Orthodox church looks like. Draw below what the outside of your church looks like. Perhaps draw a picture of your priest standing next to it. God gives us churches to attend so that we can hear priests preach His word and learn about His love for us.

God also gives us five senses and they are all engaged, or used, during our time inside of a church. What five senses did the little girl or boy in the story use while attending the funeral ceremony?

Answer:

She or he tasted koliva/sitari, held a candle, smelled incense, heard prayers, and saw icons/casket/hearse.

Here are five verses from the Bible to match our five senses:

Touch: *That which was from the beginning, which we have heard, which we have seen with our eyes, which we have looked upon, and our hands have handled, is the Word of Life*—1 John 1:1

Taste: *In the sweat of thy face shalt thou eat bread, till thou return unto the ground, for out of it wast thou taken; for dust thou art and unto dust thou shall return*—Genesis 3:19

Hear: *Very truly I tell you, a time is coming and has now come when the dead will hear the voice of the Son of God and those who hear will live*—John 5:25

See: *Precious in the sight of the Lord is the death of his Godly ones*—Psalm 116:15

Smell: *For we are unto God a sweet fragrance of Christ, in them that are saved, and in them that perish*—2 Corinthians 2:15

What is your favorite example of each of the five senses? Do you like to touch your soft teddy bear, taste ice cream, hear a choir sing, see balloons, or smell cookies baking? Draw or write out your personal favorites below:

Touch

Taste

Hear

See

Smell

VOCABULARY REVIEW:

From memory, write the definitions of the following terms in your own words:

Censer: _____

Eulogy: _____

Funeral procession: _____

Hearse: _____

Holy oil: _____

Incense: _____

Narthex: _____

Pallbearer: _____

Theotokos: _____

Venerate: _____

Now compare what you wrote with the glossary from the back of your storybook. Were you close? Good job!

Vocabulary Word Search

Look backwards, forward, up and down!

Cemetery	Grave	Tomb
Interred	Vault	Consecrate
Headstone	Crypt	Ancestors
Plaque	Mausoleum	Soul Saturday

```
S G R T H F D S A Q W X C V B N A V A L S J T Y O L M Q M
O B C F R T G B C E M E T S G H J U M C R Y P T X P Y G U
U B A N C E S T O R S P H B E G F D S K B Y B G F W Q H E
L B G F E R H Y N B W O L K Y P N B S R D A E V B N I J L
S I K J H G N B R E W F I J E N O T S D A E H H G W F X O
A K B V T Y H C X R A D O N I T S A B R F D W D Q J V P S
T L U A V N R F G H C Q E D C E M E T Q K O T O M B F A U
U P P A N I K H I D A H W Q G V C R T P A R A S T O S I A
R U H B V R T G F D E W G R A V E J R F V B T F D J K O M
D N Y H E U Q A L P U J P L A Q B Y J A O J Q L B R T N V
A H B G R T G H Y B C O N S E C R A T E B H Q A S Z X Y P
Y R E T E M E C B V E R C E F O N E Q W C I N T E R R E D
D V R B Q A C G W N Y C A E D T Y Q M O P J Z C G N D Q A
M Q L X V B N E T R D U K M O M D W X D S F B Y M U V N U
H M U E W D V C Z U O L P H B C C O N S E C R A T E T X C
S W B G T R I S A G I O N C K O L Y H G F D S A Q W E C V
B D S E J W H I D Q S X Z Y U E B H K L M K D W F V T B C
B V Y F D C Y I O R A D O N I T S A O P B V B R D S X B N
M B C E C R Y P T X O U J N G T R V C E I V Z E F V B G Y
O U H V N W C W Q G B J W D W A C Y I K N P Q A C T N N U
R X Z U K P D C W Z R V V Y I E A V A L S N V N S W S X E
```

SOLUTION TO WORD SEARCH:

```
S G R T H F D S A Q W X C V B N A V A L S J T Y O L M Q M
O B C F R T G B C E M E T S G H J U M C R Y P T X P Y G U
U B A N C E S T O R S P H B E G F D S K B Y B G F W Q H E
L B G F E R H Y N B W O L K Y P N B S R D A E V B N I J L
S I K J H G N B R E W F I J E N O T S D A E H H G W F X O
A K B V T Y H C X R A D O N I T S A B R F D W D Q J V P S
T L U A V N R F G H C Q E D C E M E T Q K O T O M B F A U
U P P A N I K H I D A H W Q G V C R T P A R A S T O S I A
R U H B V R T G F D E W G R A V E J R F V B T F D J K O M
D N Y H E U Q A L P U J P L A Q B Y J A O J Q L B R T N V
A H B G R T G H Y B C O N S E C R A T E B H Q A S Z X Y P
Y R E T E M E C B V E R C E F O N E Q W C I N T E R R E D
D V R B Q A C G W N Y C A E D T Y Q M O P J Z C G N D Q A
M Q L X V B N E T R D U K M O M D W X D S F B Y M U V N U
H M U E W D V C Z U O L P H B C C O N S E C R A T E T X C
S W B G T R I S A G I O N C K O L Y H G F D S A Q E C V
B D S E J W H I D Q S X Z Y U E B H K L M K D W F V T B C
B V Y F D C Y I O R A D O N I T S A O P B V B R D S X B N
M B C E C R Y P T X O U J N G T R V C E I V Z E F V B G Y
O U H V N W C W Q G B J W D W A C Y I K N P Q A C T N N U
R X Z U K P D C W Z R V V Y I E A V A L S N V N S W S X E
```

Have you ever been to a **cemetery**? Did you know the word is Greek in origin? What did it look like? Was it a memorial park where all of the plaques are flat to the ground, or did you see **headstones** carved from rock? Sometimes headstones are cast in concrete and sometimes wooden crosses are put up instead. With your parent's permission, Google a place called Hope Cemetery in Barre, VT. Print out some of the monuments you like best, cut them out and paste them below. The stone airplane is my favorite. What talented artists to carve so many different types of memorials for different types of people! Next, Google the resting place of your favorite saint. Are they buried or were they placed in a **tomb**?

At the cemetery, there are many ways we can show our love for the one who has fallen asleep in the Lord. Some people like to leave special outdoor candles or greeting cards, others leave small stones to show they had visited. Garden decorations such as pinwheels, solar lights, stepping stones, and statuary are also popular. Check with your cemetery to see if this is permissible. If not, create a memory garden at home and decorate this space with beautiful flowers. In the stories, the family planted flowers at the grave of their Baba or Yiayia. What are your favorite flowers? Would you like to draw a big bouquet for your loved one?

In the story, we mentioned several important dates of remembrance for Orthodox Christians. Print out "a year at a glance" calendar page. Highlight the date when someone close to you had died. Count 40 days past this date and highlight again. Highlight the date of your Slava, if applicable. Then highlight the name day of your deceased loved one. Highlight also their birthday. Highlight the anniversary date of their marriage, if applicable. Then highlight the Soul Saturdays for the year. Look at all the color on your calendar!

See how many opportunities there are to remember those who have passed away? Doesn't it make you feel better to know that they will never be forgotten? Depending on the terminology of your parish, ask your family to request a **Mnimosino/Panikhida/Parastos/Pomen**. Your priest will be very happy to perform these services in memory of your loved one. You need only give him a list of names so he knows who to commemorate.

Every New Year's Eve in the future, make it a tradition to mark these dates on the calendar again, using a different color for each deceased family member. Other ways you can remember your loved one is to offer alms in their name to the church, a monastery, or another favorite charity that was dear to their heart. You can also mention them in your daily prayers and light a candle for them each Sunday in church. What a marvelous helper you will be!

To live on in the hearts of those who loved you is to never truly die. Our hope is in Christ and we hold fast to His promise of eternal life in heaven.

Ask your helper to take out the Bible.
Together, look up verse *1 Thessalonians 4:13-14*. Copy it below:

_____
_____
_____
_____
_____
_____
_____

Next, look up and copy *Isaiah 41:10*.

_____
_____
_____
_____
_____
_____
_____

Lastly, *Matthew 5:4.*

_____
- - - - - - - - - - - - - - - -
_____
- - - - - - - - - - - - - - - -
_____
- - - - - - - - - - - - - - - -
_____
- - - - - - - - - - - - - - - -
_____
- - - - - - - - - - - - - - - -

Now that you have written and thought about the Word of God, how do you feel? Talk about these feelings with your helper. It always makes us feel better to talk.

RESOURCES

Never feel alone in your grief. God gave us Christ to be our comfort, and He gave us the Church to be our place of refuge. God also gave us helpers in our parents, priests, godparents, and friends. There are many who can help you during your time of mourning. Below are but a few resources. Remember there is no shame in sharing your feelings, even ones which are scary. The helpers in your life will never think poorly of you for expressing your deepest thoughts. Mourning is hard and helpers are everywhere!

Dr. Alan Wolfelt
Center for Love and Life Transition
3735 Broken Bow Road
Fort Collins, Colorado 80526
(970) 226-6050
info@centerforloss.com
www.centerforloss.com

The Sharing Place-Grief Support for Children
1695 East 3300 South
Salt Lake City, Utah 84106
healing@thesharingplace.com
www.thesharingplace.org

National Alliance for Grieving Children
900 SE Ocean Blvd. Suite 130D
Stuart, FL 34994
(866) 432-1542
www.nationalallianceforgrievingchildren.org

On the opposite page we see several ways we can create keepsake remembrances of our loved one. These elements were glued onto a board and placed behind glass in a shadowbox. Inside we see 5×7 memorial cards custom created at a print shop. You may choose to have an icon on one side with your loved one's photo and information or poem on the other side. You may choose to use the more traditional smaller cards offered by the funeral home, too. Next, we see lapel ribbons created for guests to wear, simply assembled with a small gold safety pin. These were kept in a basket next to the memorial cards so that they could be easily found and worn during the wake. We also see pressed petals, various floral elements from the funeral floral arrangements, and dried roses from the casket spray glued into place.

Lastly, there are round glass stones which were handed out at the cemetery to serve as a pocket touchstone. As a circle has no end, this memory stone symbolizes our unending love for the one who passed away. These can be found at the craft store in a rainbow of colors to match the favorite color of your loved one. Can you and your helpers think of any other keepsake ideas?

NOTES

www.ingramcontent.com/pod-product-compliance
Lightning Source LLC
Chambersburg PA
CBHW080519020526
44113CB00055B/2532